P9-EED-741

To:

_____

From:

_____

So This Is
How Being a
Grandmother
Feels

Chris Shea

**Andrews McMeel
Publishing**

Kansas City

ISBN-13: 978-0-7407-1939-4
ISBN-10: 0-7407-1939-4

Library of Congress
Card Number: 2001086440

Book composition by Kelly & Company

So This Is
How Being a
Grandmother
Feels

Grandbabies....

Who instructs
these
tiny
thieves

to
steal our
hearts
and
take our breath
away ?

And why
isn't it
written

anywhere

that the
first gift
we'll give
to our
grandchildren

won't be

a ducky

or a

blanket

or a new pair

of jammies.

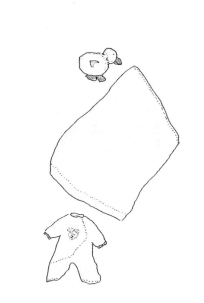

The first gift
we
give
is our
heart.

So this
is how being
a grandmother
feels...

like the
sun coming out
for the
very first
time

and the
grass growing
greener
on
your side of the
fence.

and the sky
looking bluer
than
ever
before,

because
Heaven's
come closer
to
earth.

How
could we ever
prepare
ourselves

for that moment

we long await

and plan for

and dream
of,

Nana
Grandmother
Nanny
Mimi
Mommom
Gram
Gramma . . .
What shall I be called?

because

there's no way
of knowing

how wonderful
walking on air

is going to feel.

Becoming a
grandmother
changes our
thinking.

And what
seemed like enough
long ago for our children
simply

will no longer do.

So two pairs
of sleepers
turns into six pairs
and

ten flannel blankets
are

better than three
were,

one
    little teddy bear
        isn't enough,

and a
night light
that throws stars
on the
nursery ceiling —
that's not
a luxury, really.

We're blessed
that
we're seeing
our children
as
parents,

raising
their families
with wisdom
and
love

and filling
our hearts
with
pride.

So
this
is what
being
a grandmother
is.

It's

feeling
the need

to remind
the new
mothers

to cherish
the things
they think
they won't miss,

like

tiny little fingerprints
all over
the glass;

and it's wanting
to whisper
to all the
new fathers

that

an unmowed lawn

will

always

wait.

But
childhood ...

hurries by.

This
  is what
every grandmother
     knows:

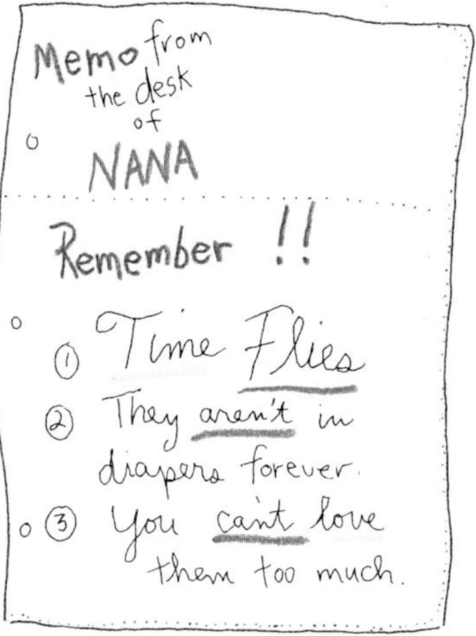
Memo from the desk of NANA
Remember !!
① Time Flies
② They aren't in diapers forever.
③ You can't love them too much.

that
granddaughters
are
poems
with
heartbeats,

that
grandsons
are
godsends
from
heaven,

and that no matter how many,

no matter
how
old,

grandchildren
continue to
take us
to places
our hearts
never
knew
were there.